WHITEHALL PUBLIC LIBRARY
36245 Park St., P.O. Box 36
Whitehall, WI 54773-0036

YOU CAN DRAW IT!
MONSTERS

WRITTEN BY JON EPPARD
ILLUSTRATED BY JOEL VOLLMER

BELLWETHER MEDIA • MINNEAPOLIS, MN

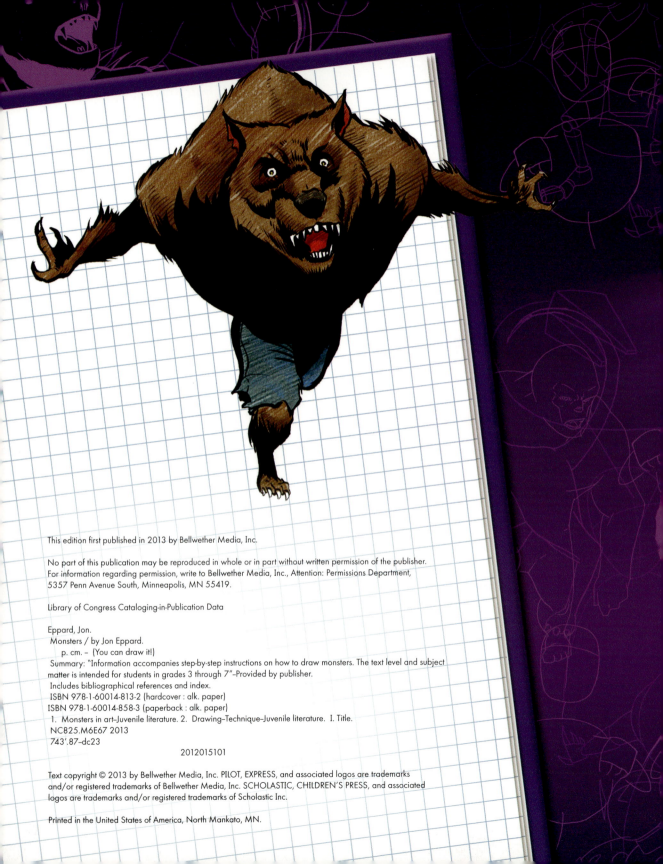

This edition first published in 2013 by Bellwether Media, Inc.

No part of this publication may be reproduced in whole or in part without written permission of the publisher. For information regarding permission, write to Bellwether Media, Inc., Attention: Permissions Department, 5357 Penn Avenue South, Minneapolis, MN 55419.

Library of Congress Cataloging-in-Publication Data

Eppard, Jon.
 Monsters / by Jon Eppard.
   p. cm. – (You can draw it!)
 Summary: "Information accompanies step-by-step instructions on how to draw monsters. The text level and subject matter is intended for students in grades 3 through 7"–Provided by publisher.
 Includes bibliographical references and index.
 ISBN 978-1-60014-813-2 (hardcover : alk. paper)
 ISBN 978-1-60014-858-3 (paperback : alk. paper)
 1. Monsters in art–Juvenile literature. 2. Drawing–Technique–Juvenile literature. I. Title.
 NC825.M6E67 2013
 743'.87–dc23
                    2012015101

Text copyright © 2013 by Bellwether Media, Inc. PILOT, EXPRESS, and associated logos are trademarks and/or registered trademarks of Bellwether Media, Inc. SCHOLASTIC, CHILDREN'S PRESS, and associated logos are trademarks and/or registered trademarks of Scholastic Inc.

Printed in the United States of America, North Mankato, MN.

TABLE OF CONTENTS

Monsters!	4
Chupacabra	6
Frankenstein's Monster	8
Goblin	10
Mummy	12
Loch Ness Monster	14
Werewolf	16
Zombie	18
Bigfoot	20
Glossary	22
To Learn More	23
Index	24

MONSTERS!

Monsters have existed in myths, **legends**, and folktales for thousands of years. While most people accept that monsters are not real, many insist that they exist. Some even claim to have encountered them. Their stories continue to raise the question: are they fact or are they fiction?

DRAWING FROM OTHER ILLUSTRATIONS IS A GREAT PLACE TO START. WORK YOUR WAY UP TO DRAWING FROM YOUR IMAGINATION.

Before you begin drawing, you will need a few basic supplies.

PAPER

DRAWING PENCILS

BLACK INK PEN

2B OR NOT 2B?

NOT ALL DRAWING PENCILS ARE THE SAME. "B" PENCILS ARE SOFTER, MAKE DARKER MARKS, AND SMUDGE EASILY. "H" PENCILS ARE HARDER, MAKE LIGHTER MARKS, AND DON'T SMUDGE VERY MUCH AT ALL.

COLORED PENCILS
(ALL DRAWINGS IN THIS BOOK WERE FINISHED WITH COLORED PENCILS.)

ERASER

PENCIL SHARPENER

Chupacabra
The Blood-Sucker

In 1995, the chupacabra spread fear in Puerto Rico. Farmers would wake in the morning to find their livestock drained of blood. The only signs of struggle were **puncture** wounds on the necks of the victims. Farmers blamed the killings on a creature with the spikes of a lizard, alien eyes, and vampire teeth. They called it *chupacabra*, or "goat sucker."

BEGIN WITH A SQUARE FOR THE HEAD AND A LARGE OVAL FOR THE BODY

ADD THE EYES, MOUTH, AND POINTED EARS

DRAW THE EDGE OF THE CURVED TAIL

BREAK IT DOWN

JUST ABOUT ANY SUBJECT YOU'RE DRAWING CAN BE BROKEN DOWN INTO SMALLER PARTS. LOOK FOR CIRCLES, OVALS, SQUARES, AND OTHER BASIC SHAPES THAT CAN HELP BUILD YOUR DRAWING.

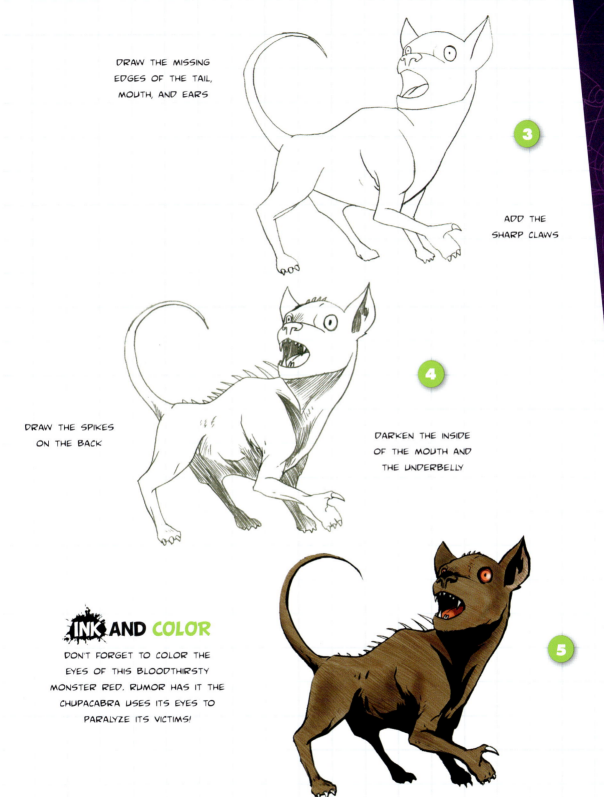

Frankenstein's Monster
The Experiment Gone Wrong

Victor Frankenstein thought he had discovered the secret of life. Then the scientist watched in horror as the monster he created took its first breath. The creature was a **repulsive** patchwork of old body parts. Victor abandoned his creation, and the lonely monster grew **vengeful**. The monster murdered Victor's loved ones and left him to be tortured by guilt.

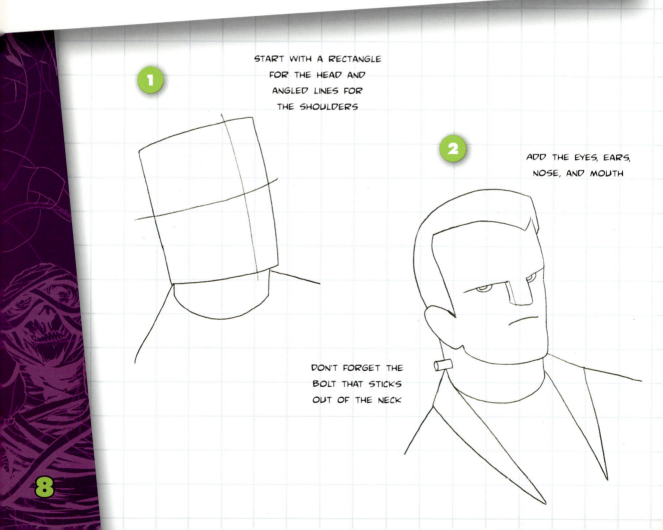

1. START WITH A RECTANGLE FOR THE HEAD AND ANGLED LINES FOR THE SHOULDERS

2. ADD THE EYES, EARS, NOSE, AND MOUTH

DON'T FORGET THE BOLT THAT STICKS OUT OF THE NECK

DRAW JAGGED LINES
TO MAKE THE HAIR
LOOK MESSY

ADD DETAIL TO THE
EARS AND EYES

ADD SCARS TO
THE FACE

ADD SHADOWS
AROUND THE EYES AND
BELOW THE CHIN

INK AND COLOR

DYE THE MONSTER'S HAIR WITH
YOUR BLACK INK PEN. COLOR ITS
SKIN YELLOWISH GREEN.

WHICH WAY TO GO?

IF YOU'RE LEFT-HANDED, START YOUR DRAWING FROM THE RIGHT. IF YOU'RE RIGHT-HANDED, START YOUR DRAWING FROM THE LEFT. THIS WILL HELP YOU AVOID SMUDGING.

Goblin
The Mischief Maker

The short, **grotesque** creatures of goblin **folklore** dwell in the darkness of caves and forests. When they come out, it is to cause mischief in the homes of humans. These clever pranksters spook sleeping families by banging on pots and pans, moving furniture, and pounding on walls and doors. Some even show up to punish children who misbehave!

1. START WITH A STICK FIGURE
USE AN EGG SHAPE FOR THE HEAD AND SQUARES FOR HANDS

2. USE CIRCLES AND RECTANGLES TO BUILD THE BODY

Mummy
The Curse Bearer

The mummy of ancient Egypt's King Tut rested in peace until explorers discovered his **tomb** in the 1920s. After that, strange things started happening. Many believe that the explorers had unleashed the Mummy's Curse. Does such a curse exist? To be safe, tread lightly around tombs and graves. Even **skeptics** know not to disrupt the deep sleep of death.

1. DRAW SQUARES FOR HANDS

BEGIN WITH TWO ROUNDED SHAPES FOR THE HEAD AND BODY

2. LIGHTLY DRAW THE EYES, NOSE, AND MOUTH

ADD FINGERS TO THE HANDS

Loch Ness Monster
The Creature of the Deep

Nestled in Scotland's rugged highlands are Loch Ness and its legendary monster. Over the centuries, thousands of people have claimed to see the lake's glassy surface broken by a dark form. Others have glimpsed a shadowy creature beneath the surface. So far, no one has been able to prove that an **aquatic** monster exists. Until someone can, the depths of Loch Ness will contain a mystery.

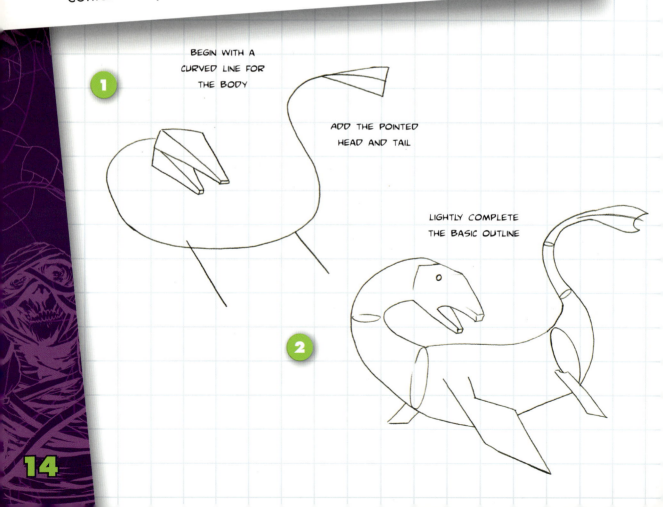

1. BEGIN WITH A CURVED LINE FOR THE BODY
   ADD THE POINTED HEAD AND TAIL
2. LIGHTLY COMPLETE THE BASIC OUTLINE

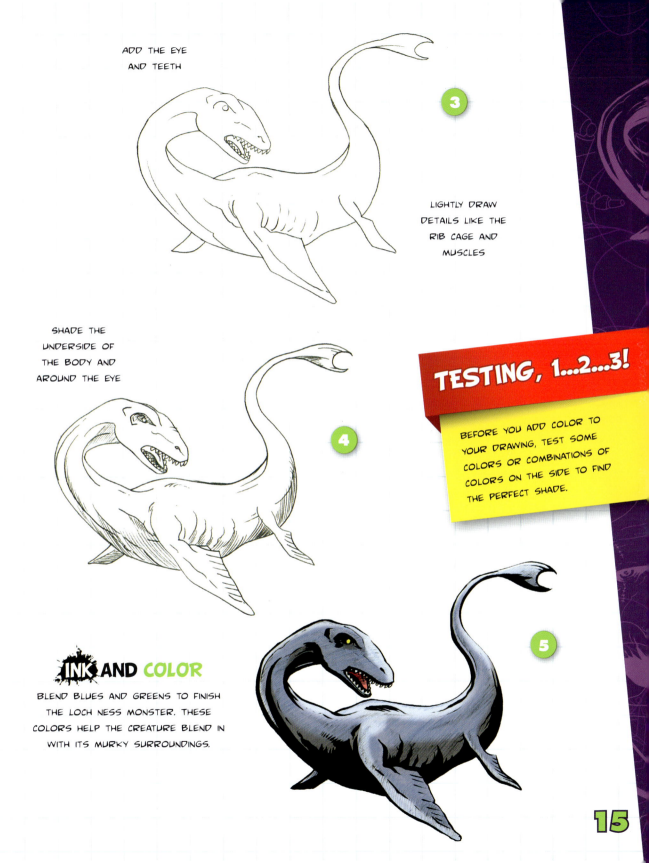

ADD THE EYE AND TEETH

3

LIGHTLY DRAW DETAILS LIKE THE RIB CAGE AND MUSCLES

SHADE THE UNDERSIDE OF THE BODY AND AROUND THE EYE

4

TESTING, 1...2...3!

BEFORE YOU ADD COLOR TO YOUR DRAWING, TEST SOME COLORS OR COMBINATIONS OF COLORS ON THE SIDE TO FIND THE PERFECT SHADE.

INK AND COLOR

BLEND BLUES AND GREENS TO FINISH THE LOCH NESS MONSTER. THESE COLORS HELP THE CREATURE BLEND IN WITH ITS MURKY SURROUNDINGS.

5

Werewolf
The Lunar Beast

In the **Middle Ages**, cases of gruesome murder and **cannibalism** were thought to be the work of werewolves. Rumor had it that these fearsome creatures would transform at will and set out in search of flesh. Do half-humans, half-beasts prowl the dark edges of forests today? Beware of those with long fingernails, hairy palms, and a craving for raw meat!

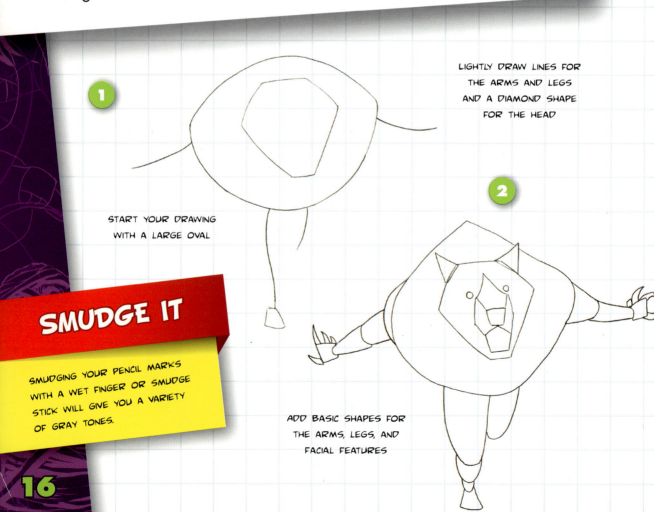

1. START YOUR DRAWING WITH A LARGE OVAL

LIGHTLY DRAW LINES FOR THE ARMS AND LEGS AND A DIAMOND SHAPE FOR THE HEAD

2. ADD BASIC SHAPES FOR THE ARMS, LEGS, AND FACIAL FEATURES

SMUDGE IT

SMUDGING YOUR PENCIL MARKS WITH A WET FINGER OR SMUDGE STICK WILL GIVE YOU A VARIETY OF GRAY TONES.

ADD DETAIL TO THE EYES AND EARS

3

DRAW THE LARGE TEETH INSIDE THE MOUTH

ADD HAIR TO THE ARMS AND CLAWS TO THE FEET

4

SHADE THE UNDERSIDE OF THE BODY AND AROUND THE EYES, EARS, AND NOSE

5

INK AND COLOR

USE NATURAL FUR COLORS FOR THE WEREWOLF. BROWN, GRAY, OR BLACK WILL MAKE THIS WOLF-MAN LOOK REAL.

Zombie
The Walking Dead

You can seal your doors and board your windows, but it's only a matter of time until they come. It's the zombie **apocalypse**, and the streets are crawling with the **undead**. Where there is life, the zombies will go. The strongest locks won't keep them from the flesh of the living. There will be no survivors.

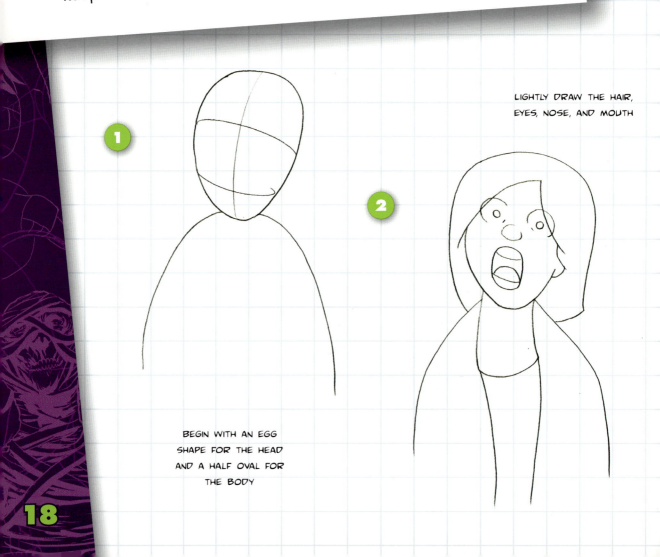

1. BEGIN WITH AN EGG SHAPE FOR THE HEAD AND A HALF OVAL FOR THE BODY

2. LIGHTLY DRAW THE HAIR, EYES, NOSE, AND MOUTH

ADD DETAIL TO THE CLOTHES AND HAIR

③

ADD TEETH AND CIRCLES AROUND THE EYES

④

ADD THE NECKLACE, TORN CLOTHES, AND BLOOD AROUND THE MOUTH

USE YOUR ARM

DRAW WITH YOUR WHOLE ARM, NOT JUST YOUR WRIST AND FINGERS.

 **AND COLOR**

USE PALE COLORS TO FINISH THE ZOMBIE'S DEAD FLESH. YOU'LL WANT A BRIGHT COLOR THAT POPS FOR THE INTENSE EYES OF A FLESH-HUNGRY MONSTER.

⑤

Bigfoot
The Forest Fright

Some people find giant footprints in the woods. Others report grunting sounds coming from behind trees. Many can only describe a feeling of being watched. A number of people, however, claim to have seen the beast itself. They return from the forest with blurry photos of a tall, hairy figure. Is this **evidence** that Bigfoot exists? The real question may be, *where will it turn up next?*

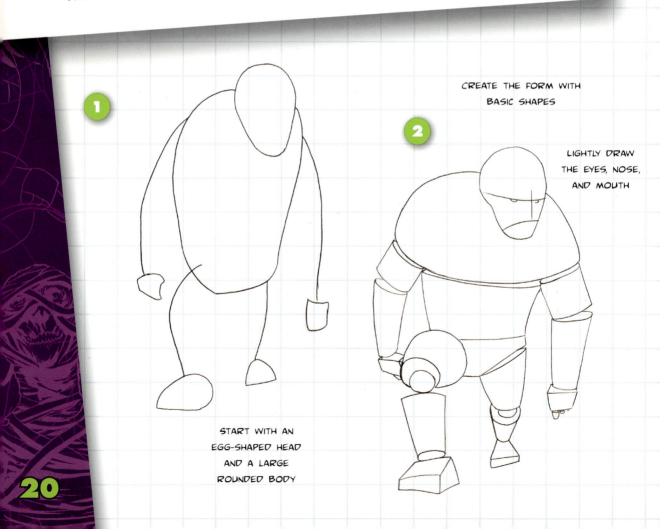

1. START WITH AN EGG-SHAPED HEAD AND A LARGE ROUNDED BODY

2. CREATE THE FORM WITH BASIC SHAPES

LIGHTLY DRAW THE EYES, NOSE, AND MOUTH

CONNECT THE BASIC SHAPES TO FORM THE OUTLINE

3

ADD DETAIL TO THE FACE, HANDS, AND FEET

4

DRAW THE FUR WITH A LOT OF SHORT LINES

MIX AND MATCH

YOU CAN MIX COLORS BY GOING OVER A PREVIOUSLY COLORED SECTION WITH A NEW COLOR.

5

INK AND COLOR

BLEND BROWN AND BLACK TO FINISH BIGFOOT'S FUR. USE A LIGHTER COLOR FOR ITS FACE, HANDS, AND FEET.

apocalypse—a disaster of unearthly nature

aquatic—living in water

cannibalism—the eating of an animal by a member of the same species

evidence—physical proof

folklore—stories, customs, and beliefs that are handed down from one generation to the next

grotesque—ugly or unnatural

legends—stories from the past; legends are widely accepted but cannot be proven as fact.

Middle Ages—a time period in Europe lasting from the 500s to the 1500s

puncture—a hole that has been pierced into something

repulsive—disgusting to the senses

skeptics—people who doubt the truth or existence of something

tomb—a chamber for the dead

undead—the dead that behave as though they are alive

vengeful—seeking revenge

TO LEARN MORE

At the Library

Mousse, Marion. *Frankenstein*. New York, N.Y.: Papercutz, 2009.

Stine, R.L. *The Curse of the Mummy's Tomb*. Milwaukee, Wisc.: Gareth Stevens Pub., 1997.

Wagner, Lloyd S. *El Chupacabras: Trail of the Goatsucker*. Lincoln, Neb.: iUniverse, Inc., 2004.

On the Web

Learning more about monsters is as easy as 1, 2, 3.

1. Go to www.factsurfer.com.

2. Enter "monsters" into the search box.

3. Click the "Surf" button and you will see a list of related Web sites.

With factsurfer.com, finding more information is just a click away.

INDEX

adding details, 11
Bigfoot, 20-21
chupacabra, 6-7
drawing from illustrations, 4
drawing lightly, 5, 13
Frankenstein's Monster, 8-9
goblin, 10-11
left-handed, 9
Loch Ness Monster, 14-15
mixing colors, 21
mummy, 12-13
right-handed, 9
smudging, 5, 9, 16
supplies, 5
testing colors, 15
using basic shapes, 6
using your arm, 19
werewolf, 16-17
zombie, 18-19